Yellow Umbrella Books are published by Capstone Press
151 Good Counsel Drive, P.O. Box 669, Mankato, Minnesota 56002
http://www.capstone-press.com

Library of Congress Cataloging-in-Publication Data
Trumbauer, Lisa, 1963–
    About 100 years ago/by Lisa Trumbauer.
    p. cm.
    Includes index.
    ISBN 0-7368-0736-5
    1. Manners and customs—History—19th century—Juvenile literature. 2. United States—
Social life and customs—19th century—Juvenile literature. [1. United States—History—20th
century. 2. United States—Social life and customs—20th century.] I. Title: About one hundred
years ago. II. Title.
GT85.T78   2001
306'.0973—dc21   00-038164

    Summary: Describes what clothes, cars, bicycles, cities, and sports were like 100 years ago.

Editorial Credits:
Susan Evento, Managing Editor/Product Development; Elizabeth Jaffe, Senior Editor;
    Sydney Wright and Charles Hunt, Designers; Kimberly Danger and Heidi Schoof,
    Photo Researchers

Photo Credits:
Cover: FPG International LLC; Title Page (clockwise from top left) Ingram Collection/Archive
Photos, International Stock/Earl Kogler, DeWitt Historical Society/Archive Photos, Visuals
Unlimited/Mark E. Gibson; Page 2: Visuals Unlimited/Jeff J. Daly (left), Ingram
Collection/Archive Photos (right); Page 3: Unicorn Stock Photos/Tommy Dodson (left), FPG
International LLC (right); Page 4: McNee Photos/FPG International LLC ; Page 5: International
Stock/Earl Kogler; Page 6: Visuals Unlimited (left), Visuals Unlimited/Mark E. Gibson (right);
Page 7: Unicorn Stock Photos/A. Gurmankin (left), Archive Photos (inset); Page 8: Visuals
Unlimited/Jeff J. Daly, FPG International LLC (inset); Page 9: Mark Reinstein/Pictor; Page 10:
Photo Network; Page 11: Peter Gridley/FPG International LLC; Page 12: FPG International
LLC; Page 13: Unicorn Stock Photos/Andre Jenny; Page 14: DeWitt Historical Society/Archive
Photos (top), Visuals Unlimited/Mark E. Gibson (bottom); Page 15: Photri-Microstock; Page 16:
Arthur Tilley/FPG International LLC

1 2 3 4 5 6 06 05 04 03 02 01

About 100 Years Ago

By Lisa Trumbauer

Consulting Editor: Gail Saunders-Smith, Ph.D.
Consultants: Claudine Jellison and
Patricia Williams, Reading Recovery Teachers
Content Consultant: Andrew Gyory, Ph.D., American History

Yellow Umbrella Books

an imprint of Capstone Press
Mankato, Minnesota

Let's see how people and things about 100 years ago were different from people and things today.

About 100 years ago, girls wore only dresses. Boys wore short pants called knickers.

These are clothes today.

How have clothes changed?

If you lived about 100 years ago, you may have gone for a bike ride.

Today, you also may go
for a bike ride.

How are the bicycles
and clothes alike?
How are they different?

Did you know that
about 100 years ago
people played sports?

How do sports teams today look different from the teams of about 100 years ago?

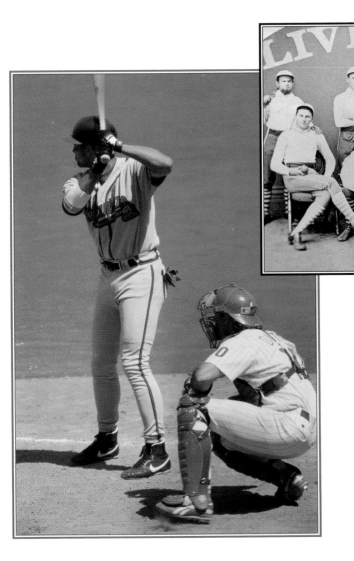

About 100 years ago,
some people drove cars.
Most cars were black.

People had to hand-crank cars
to get them started.
Cars did not go very fast.

This is a car today.
How have cars changed?
How have cars
stayed the same?

About 100 years ago,
people were learning
how to build simple planes.
Only one person could sit
in these planes.
They did not fly very far.

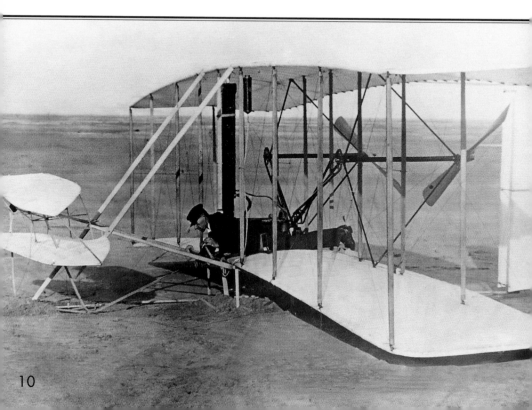

Today, many people can fly
at one time.
Many things are brought
from place to place by plane.
Planes go all over the world.

Here is a city
about 100 years ago.
Most buildings
were not very tall.

Here is the same city today.
There are more buildings, and
most of the buildings are tall.

Here is a boy
in school about
100 years ago.

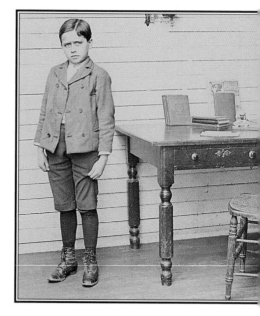

Here are
children in
school today.

How do you think children did
schoolwork 100 years ago?

Here is a family having
a picnic about 100 years ago.

This is a family
having a picnic today.
Many things have changed.
What has stayed the same?

Words to Know/Index

bicycle—a vehicle with two wheels that is ridden by pedaling and steering handlebars; page 5

building—a structure with walls and a roof; pages 12, 13

change—to make different or to become different; pages 3, 9, 16

different—not the same; pages 2, 5, 7

family—a group of people who are related, especially parents and their children; pages 15, 16

hand-crank—to turn a crank using the hands to start something; a crank is a handle that is attached to a shaft; page 8

knickers—short, loose pants that end just below the knee; page 2

picnic—a short trip to eat a meal outdoors; pages 15, 16

sport—a game or activity played for exercise or pleasure; pages 6, 7

team—a group of people who work or play together; page 7

Word Count: 278
Early-Intervention Levels: 13–16